MW01178546

The Legacy Tree

A Memoir

In loving memory of my father, George

This book was created to preserve the
memories and experiences of

_____,

so that they can be cherished and
shared for generations to come.

1. What is your full name, and were you named after anyone?

_____

_____

_____

_____

_____

_____

2. What is your date of birth?

_____

_____

_____

_____

_____

3. Where were you born (city, address, name of hospital, etc.)?

_____

_____

_____

_____

_____

_____

4. What is/ was your mother's full name? Your father's full name?

_____

_____

_____

_____

_____

5. What is your lucky number, and why? Has it ever brought you luck?

_____

_____

_____

_____

6. What is your favourite colour?

_____

_____

_____

_____

7. What is your favourite movie of all time and why?

_____

_____

_____

_____

_____

_____

_____

8. What is your favourite song? Does it hold any sentimental meaning?

_____

_____

_____

_____

_____

_____

_____

9. How old were you when you bought/ received your first vehicle? Describe it.

_____

_____

_____

_____

_____

10. Of all the vehicles you've ever owned, which one was your favourite?

_____

_____

_____

11. If you could afford any vehicle in the world, what would it be?

_____

_____

_____

_____

12. As a child, what did you want to be when you grew up? Did anyone inspire this?

_____

_____

_____

_____

_____

_____

_____

13. With your knowledge and experience now, if you could have done any job in the world, what would it have been and why?

_____

_____

_____

_____

_____

_____

_____

14. What is your favourite place in the world that you've visited? Why?

_____

_____

_____

_____

15. If you could afford to travel anywhere in the world, where would you go? What would you like to do there?

_____

_____

_____

_____

16. Did you have any pets as a child? What was your favourite?

_____

_____

_____

_____

17. What was the most difficult part of your childhood?

_____

_____

_____

_____

_____

_____

_____

18. What was your favourite meal that your mother or father (or anyone) prepared for you as a child?

_____

_____

_____

_____

_____

_____

_____

19. Write out your favourite recipe (or two).

_____

_____

_____

_____

_____

_____

_____

_____

_____

_____

_____

_____

_____

_____

_____

20. What is your favourite holiday and why?

_____

_____

_____

_____

_____

_____

_____

_____

21. What has been your favourite age so far in life and why?

_____

_____

_____

_____

_____

_____

_____

_____

22. Describe in detail your most cherished childhood memory.

_____

_____

_____

_____

_____

_____

_____

_____

_____

_____

_____

_____

_____

_____

_____

_____

23. Who was your first kiss with? When was it?

_____

_____

_____

_____

_____

24. Who was your first boyfriend/girlfriend?

_____

_____

_____

_____

25. What qualities do you feel are most important in a partner/spouse?

_____

_____

_____

_____

_____

26. Describe when, how and where you and your partner/spouse met. What was your first impression?

_____

_____

_____

_____

_____

_____

_____

27. How did your spouse propose to you, or how did you propose to your spouse?

_____

_____

_____

_____

_____

_____

_____

28. Describe your wedding day (the date, who stood up for you, how many attended, etc.).

_____

_____

_____

_____

_____

_____

_____

_____

_____

_____

_____

_____

_____

_____

29. Are there any experiences you've not yet had that you regret not having? What are they?

_____

_____

_____

_____

_____

_____

_____

30. who was your best friend in school and what was the best thing about him or her?

_____

_____

_____

_____

_____

_____

_____

31. What qualities are most important in a good friend?

_____

_____

_____

_____

32. What is your worst habit?

_____

_____

_____

_____

33. What is your biggest fear?

_____

_____

_____

_____

34. What is your favourite feature about yourself? What do you wish you could change?

_____

_____

_____

_____

35. If you could look like any movie star, singer or famous artist, who would it be?

_____

_____

_____

_____

36. Did you enjoy your school days? Why or why not?

_____

_____

_____

_____

_____

_____

_____

37. Who was the best teacher you've ever had, and who was the worst? Explain.

_____

_____

_____

_____

_____

_____

38. Did you have a nickname growing up? If so, what was it and how did you get it?

_____

_____

_____

_____

_____

_____

_____

39. How do you think your peers in school would have described you back then?

_____

_____

_____

_____

_____

_____

40. What was your favourite subject in school? What was your least favourite?

_____

_____

_____

_____

_____

_____

41. What are the names and locations of all the schools you attended?

_____

_____

_____

_____

_____

_____

_____

_____

_____

_____

42. Who was the strictest when you were growing up?

_____

_____

_____

_____

_____

_____

_____

43. What are your fondest memories of your mother?

_____

_____

_____

_____

_____

_____

_____

44. What are your fondest memories of your father?

_____

_____

_____

_____

_____

_____

_____

45. What is/was your relationship like with your parents?

_____

_____

_____

_____

_____

_____

_____

_____

_____

46. What toy did you wish for as a child that you never did receive?

_____

_____

_____

_____

_____

47. What is the biggest disappointment that you can remember having as a child?

_____

_____

_____

_____

_____

_____

_____

48. Did you belong to any clubs throughout your youth?

_____

_____

_____

_____

_____

_____

_____

_____

49. What have been the three happiest moments in your life so far?

50. Have you ever been arrested? If so, explain. If not, is there anything you've done that you would have been in big trouble for if someone had found out?

_____

_____

_____

_____

_____

51. What is your favourite book and/or author?

_____

_____

_____

_____

52. If you won the lottery, what would you do with the money?

_____

_____

_____

_____

53. What is the most embarrassing thing that has ever happened to you?

_____

_____

_____

_____

_____

54. What really gives you the creeps?

_____

_____

_____

55. What is the best gift you've ever received?

_____

_____

_____

_____

_____

56. What is the bravest thing you've ever done?

_____

_____

_____

_____

57. Do you agree with the death penalty? Why or why not?

_____

_____

_____

_____

_____

58. When you were young were you involved in any type of political protests?

_____

_____

_____

_____

59. Did you ever run away from home? If so, why, and where did you go?

_____

_____

_____

_____

_____

_____

60. What is the most trouble you were ever in as a child, and what did you do?

_____

_____

_____

_____

_____

_____

_____

61. Did you collect anything when you were younger (rocks, stamps, etc.)?

_____

_____

_____

62. Were you involved in any sports, music lessons, etc. as a child?

_____

_____

_____

63. What are/ were your grandparents full names, birth dates and places of birth?

_____

_____

_____

_____

_____

_____

64. What are/ were your parents occupations?

_____

_____

_____

_____

_____

_____

_____

65. What made you pursue the career you chose?

_____

_____

_____

_____

_____

_____

_____

_____

66. Can you remember all of the places you've worked, including your first job? List as many as you can think of.

_____

_____

_____

_____

_____

_____

_____

_____

_____

_____

_____

_____

_____

_____

67. What are the most memorable family vacations that you can recall?

_____

_____

_____

_____

_____

_____

_____

68. Are there any sad times or memories that you'd like to share?

_____

_____

_____

_____

_____

_____

_____

69. Are there any specific moments or experiences that you would consider as true breakthroughs in your life?

_____

_____

_____

_____

_____

_____

_____

_____

70. If you could go back and do one thing differently, what would it be and why?

_____

_____

_____

_____

_____

_____

_____

71. What are some of the most important lessons you've learned in life?

_____

_____

_____

_____

_____

_____

_____

72. What are you most grateful for in your life?

_____

_____

_____

_____

_____

_____

_____

73. Share the funniest family story (or stories) you can remember.

_____

_____

_____

_____

_____

_____

_____

_____

_____

_____

_____

_____

_____

_____

74. Do you remember what you were doing when John F Kennedy was shot? When 9/11 occurred?

_____

_____

_____

_____

_____

_____

_____

75. Have you ever met anyone famous?

_____

_____

_____

_____

_____

_____

_____

76. What is your favourite memory so far involving your child/ children?

_____

_____

_____

_____

_____

_____

_____

77. What advice would you give about raising children?

_____

_____

_____

_____

_____

_____

_____

78. Describe the house you grew up in. Were there any special places or items in the house that stand out in your memory?

_____

_____

_____

_____

_____

_____

_____

79. What was the neighbourhood like where you grew up?

_____

_____

_____

_____

_____

_____

_____

_____

80. Can you remember all of the places you've lived, including your first address? List as many as you can think of.

_____

_____

_____

_____

_____

_____

_____

_____

_____

_____

_____

_____

_____

_____

81. What skills or talents do you feel you learned or inherited from your parents?

_____

_____

_____

_____

_____

_____

_____

82. Would you say you are more like your mother or your father? In what ways?

_____

_____

_____

_____

_____

_____

_____

83. If they are gone, how did your parents pass away? Where are they buried?

_____

_____

_____

_____

_____

_____

_____

84. Is there anything you regret not asking your parents?

_____

_____

_____

_____

_____

_____

_____

_____

85. What games do you remember playing with family or friends when growing up?

_____

_____

_____

_____

_____

86. Name some trends or fads you remember when growing up (fashion, hair styles, etc.).

_____

_____

_____

_____

_____

87. How did you choose your child's/ children's names?

_____

_____

_____

_____

_____

88. What are your proudest moments so far in your life?

_____

_____

_____

_____

_____

_____

89. Are there any special family traditions that have been passed down through generations?

_____

_____

_____

_____

_____

_____

_____

_____

90. What was your favourite TV show, cartoon or movie as a child?

_____

_____

_____

91. Do you have a secret with your siblings or best friends that your parents never found out about?

_____

_____

_____

92. Is there anything about your child/children that reminds you of yourself at their age?

_____

_____

_____

_____

93. Do you believe in love at first sight?

_____

_____

_____

_____

_____

94. Who has had the biggest influence on you in your life? Why and in what ways?

_____

_____

_____

_____

_____

_____

95. What is your favourite meal?

_____

_____

_____

_____

96. What would you say is your guilty pleasure?

_____

_____

_____

_____

_____

_____

97. What is the key to a happy and successful marriage?

_____

_____

_____

_____

_____

_____

_____

_____

_____

98. What are your greatest strengths?

_____

_____

_____

_____

_____

_____

_____

99. What are your weaknesses?

_____

_____

_____

_____

_____

_____

_____

100. In your opinion, what are the best words to live by?

_____

_____

_____

_____

_____

_____

_____

101. How would you like to be remembered?

_____

_____

_____

_____

_____

_____

_____

Use this space for extra notes, personal questions or special photos.

Use this space for extra notes, personal questions or special photos.